DOOMED HIST

MISSION EXPLOSIONS!

The *Challenger* Space Shuttle, 1986 and the *Columbia* Space Shuttle, 2003

by Anne O'Daly

BEARPORT
PUBLISHING

Minneapolis, Minnesota

Credits: Front Cover: ©Everett Historical/Shutterstock; 1, ©NASA; 3, ©JSC/NASA; 4–5, ©NASA; 6, © NASA; 7, ©DFRC/Tony Landis/NASA; 8, ©NASA; 9, ©Brian Donovan/NASA; 10, ©JSC/NASA; 11, ©JSC/NASA; 12, ©Everett Collection Historical/Alamy; 13, ©KSC/NASA; 14, ©KSC/NASA; 15, ©NASA; 16, ©Archives/NASA; 17, ©KSC/NASA; 18-19, ©NASA; 20, ©JSC/NASA; 21, ©HSFG/NASA; 22, ©NASA; 23, ©KSC/NASA; 24, ©JSC/NASA; 25, ©JSC/NASA; 26, ©KSC/NASA; 27, ©James E Scarborough/Public Domain; 28, ©NASA; 29, ©KSC/NASA.

Bearport Publishing Company Product Development Team
President: Jen Jenson; Director of Product Development: Spencer Brinker; Senior Editor: Allison Juda; Editor: Charly Haley; Associate Editor: Naomi Reich; Senior Designer: Colin O'Dea; Associate Designer: Elena Klinkner; Associate Designer: Kayla Eggert; Product Development Assistant: Anita Stasson

Brown Bear Books
Children's Publisher: Anne O'Daly; Design Manager: Keith Davis; Picture Manager: Sophie Mortimer

Library of Congress Cataloging-in-Publication Data is available at www.loc.gov or upon request from the publisher.

ISBN: 979-8-88509-396-5 (hardcover)
ISBN: 979-8-88509-518-1 (paperback)
ISBN: 979-8-88509-633-1 (ebook)

© 2023 Brown Bear Books

This edition is published by arrangement with Brown Bear Books.

For more information, write to Bearport Publishing, 5357 Penn Avenue South, Minneapolis, MN 55419.

CONTENTS

DISASTERS IN SPACE

It was a cold morning at the Kennedy Space Center in Florida, where the **astronauts** of the space shuttle *Challenger* had been waiting for days to set off into space. Finally, on January 28, 1986, it was time to go.

Large crowds gathered at the space center, and many more were watching on television. Hundreds of thousands of children tuned in, excited to see the first schoolteacher to travel into space. But just 73 seconds after liftoff, *Challenger* exploded. No one on board survived.

Another Tragedy

Officials began investigating the *Challenger* explosion immediately, and the U.S. space shuttle program was stopped for nearly three years so it could be made safer. However, 15 years later, another tragedy struck. The *Columbia* shuttle was due to land on February 1, 2003. But as the shuttle reentered Earth's **atmosphere**, it broke into pieces, killing everyone on board. The shuttle program was shut down again.

Nobody knew anything would go wrong when the space shuttle *Challenger* took off from Cape Canaveral, Florida, on its final flight.

SPACE SHUTTLE SUCCESS

Challenger was the first disaster in a shuttle program that had been running safely for years.

Space shuttles were the world's first reusable spacecraft. They took off like rockets and landed like airplanes. The U.S. space agency, called the National **Aeronautics** and Space Administration (NASA), started its shuttle program in 1972. Just four years later, the first shuttle, *Enterprise*, was finished. This vehicle never went into space. Instead, it was used to run tests and to plan for future **missions**.

Space shuttles sat on a large orange fuel tank during liftoff. Two rocket **boosters** were located on the sides.

Space Transportation

The main goal of the shuttle program was to carry equipment to and from space. The first shuttle to be launched into space was *Columbia*. It left Earth in April 1981. By 1986, there had been nine more shuttle missions.

Every shuttle had three main parts. The crew lived and worked in the **orbiter**. This part also held equipment. Two rocket boosters provided the power to get the shuttle off the ground. And a large external fuel tank—the only part of the shuttle system that was not reusable—held liquid fuel for the takeoff and **ascent**.

THE *CHALLENGER* DISASTER

Five years after the first space shuttle mission, the public had become less interested in every new launch. However, the *Challenger* mission was different. It would carry a teacher aboard.

Christa McAuliffe, a 37-year-old high school teacher from New Hampshire, had been chosen out of 11,000 applicants for the Teacher in Space Project. McAuliffe spent months training with NASA to get ready for the mission. People around the country followed her progress closely.

Part of McAuliffe's training was to prepare for the weightlessness astronauts experience in space.

Doomed from the Start?

Challenger's main task on this mission was to put satellites into space so astronomers could study Halley's Comet. Early preparations for launch had been going smoothly, but as the liftoff date approached, things started to go wrong. The launch had been planned for January 22, but problems with machinery and bad weather delayed it until January 28.

Halley's Comet last passed by Earth in 1986.

HALLEY'S COMET

A comet is a large lump of ice, dust, and rock that circles the sun. When a comet gets close to the sun, its ice melts and turns into gas, forming a long tail that trails behind the comet. Halley's Comet passes near Earth every 75 years.

9

The Crew

Challenger's crew was led by mission commander Francis "Dick" Scobee, who was on his second spaceflight. Before training as an astronaut, Scobee had flown planes for the U.S. Air Force during the Vietnam War (1955–1975) and had been a **test pilot**. Mike Smith, the shuttle's pilot and second-in-command, was on his first spaceflight.

Mission specialists Ellison Onizuka, Judith Resnick, and Ronald McNair were also part of the crew. They were aboard to help maintain the craft, launch the satellite, and run experiments.

To Study and Teach

The last two members of the *Challenger* crew were known as **payload specialists**. Gregory Jarvis was a satellite engineer whose mission assignment was to study how liquids behaved in space. The second payload specialist was McAuliffe. She would be helping with experiments and broadcasting lessons from the shuttle to schools.

McAuliffe became an instant celebrity when she was chosen to join the *Challenger* mission.

A Freezing Cold Launch

The night before *Challenger*'s launch was very cold, and a thick layer of ice had formed on the launchpad. The temperature at the time of the launch was 26 degrees Fahrenheit (−3 degrees Celsius), which was far colder than it had been for any previous launch. Some of the engineers were worried about the effect of the cold weather on the craft's O-rings—parts that sealed the rocket boosters. But the launch went ahead as scheduled.

Icicles formed on the launch tower the night before liftoff.

Explosion

Just after liftoff, dark smoke appeared from the right rocket booster, a sign that one of the O-rings had failed. Flames from the booster escaped through the **seal** and burned a hole in the fuel tank, igniting the gas and causing an explosion. The shuttle blew into pieces and fell into the Atlantic Ocean.

A ball of gas appeared in the sky seconds after *Challenger* broke up.

WATCHING A DISASTER

Teacher Kathleen Alley had taken her students to watch the *Challenger* launch in person. "That day, I stood on the lawn outside looking expectantly into the sky with 33 students. We were all waiting excitedly, and the children squealed with delight when the *Challenger* came into view on the horizon. Then, we noticed the white smoke and the split Y pattern in the sky. I knew in my heart something was dreadfully wrong."

THE *COLUMBIA* DISASTER

Seventeen years after the *Challenger* disaster, another space shuttle experienced an unbearable tragedy.

Columbia was the first space shuttle to fly into space, and by 2003 it had completed 27 successful missions. Its 28th was focused on scientific research. After a successful launch, the crew worked hard to perform more than 80 experiments in space. *Columbia* was due to complete its mission and return home on February 1. The crew prepared for reentry into Earth's atmosphere.

Columbia astronaut Kalpana Chawla performed experiments during her time in space.

NASA's Mission Control Center monitored the technical aspects of the mission and communicated with astronauts on the spacecraft.

Mission Control

The shuttle's return flight was being guided by NASA Mission Control in Houston, Texas. Just before 9:00 a.m., Mission Control noticed problems with the temperature on the shuttle's left wing, so it sent an alert to the astronauts. The shuttle commander's response was cut off. Mission Control thought communications had been briefly interrupted. When they couldn't get back in contact with *Columbia*, however, they knew something was seriously wrong. They would soon find out the craft had broken apart.

The *Columbia* crew: *(back row, from left)* David Brown, William McCool, Michael Anderson, *(front row, from left)* Kalpana Chawla, Rick Husband, Laurel Clark, Ilan Ramon.

The Crew

The commander of the *Columbia* crew was Rick Husband, an Air Force test pilot selected to join NASA's space program in 1994. His second-in-command was pilot William "Willie" McCool, who was flying his first shuttle mission. Two of the mission specialists aboard were David Brown and Laurel Clark. They were doctors doing experiments on how the human body is affected by the weightlessness of space.

A Range of Experience

The last mission specialist, Kalpana Chawla, also served as *Columbia*'s flight engineer. The payload specialists for the mission were Michael Anderson and Ilan Ramon. Anderson had been in the Air Force before he joined NASA and was in charge of dozens of science experiments on *Columbia*. Ramon, a former pilot in the Israel Air Force, was studying the effect of dust storms on climate.

People left flowers to honor *Columbia*'s seven astronauts.

Problem at Liftoff

Columbia did not break apart until it reentered Earth's atmosphere. Just like *Challenger*, however, the problem had been caused at liftoff. A piece of insulation foam had broken away from the fuel tank, hitting the shuttle's left wing. NASA engineers didn't think the foam had done much. In fact, the foam had caused serious damage to *Columbia's* nose and wing that were supposed to protect the shuttle from heat. A hole in the craft's tiles let hot gases into the shuttle during reentry, ultimately causing *Columbia* to burst into pieces.

Lost Contact

Columbia was about 200,000 feet (61,000 m) above Dallas, Texas, when Mission Control lost contact with it. Meanwhile, reports coming in from elsewhere in Texas described a booming noise and metal falling from the sky. At 9:12 a.m., when *Columbia* should have been making its final approach to the landing strip, Mission Control heard that a TV station was broadcasting footage of the shuttle breaking apart in the sky.

Insulation tiles on *Columbia* were designed to absorb extreme heat as the shuttle reentered the atmosphere.

SEEING THE PIECES

Benjamin Laster watched the doomed shuttle flying overhead. "As we saw *Columbia* coming over, we saw a lot of light, and it looked like **debris** and stuff was coming off the shuttle. We saw large masses of pieces coming off the shuttle as it was coming by . . . and then we saw a big continuous puff of vapor or smoke stream come out, and then we noticed a big chunk go over."

HARD LESSONS LEARNED

After both shuttle accidents, teams went out to look for pieces of the destroyed spacecraft.

The search for *Challenger* debris lasted from February until August of 1986. Members of the U.S. Navy collected more than 15 tons (14 t) of debris and carefully measured, photographed, and labeled each item.

On March 7, two divers found a large section of *Challenger*'s crew cabin on the ocean floor. The astronauts' remains were given to their families or buried at Arlington National Cemetery.

Navy divers found part of *Challenger*'s right wing 70 ft (20 m) below the ocean's surface.

Pieces of *Columbia* were laid on a blue outline of the shuttle to show which part of the vehicle they came from.

Metal from the Sky

Parts of *Columbia* had rained down over Texas, Louisiana, and Arkansas. Thousands of people found pieces of the shuttle in their backyards. Everyone was warned not to touch these pieces in case they had harmful chemicals. It took four months for NASA to collect the more than 82,000 pieces of *Columbia*, some as small as a nickel. The pieces were taken to Kennedy Space Center and laid out on the floor of a massive **hangar** so engineers could try to figure out what had gone wrong.

What Actually Happened

To find out what caused the *Challenger* disaster, investigators sifted through the debris of the destroyed shuttle. The horrified spectators had thought they'd seen *Challenger* explode instantly. In fact, researchers discovered that after the fuel tank collapsed, the orbiter was pulled apart by strong **aerodynamic forces.** Pieces of it, including the crew's cabin, fell into the ocean. Experts think the astronauts survived the shuttle's break up but then quickly blacked out and died from lack of oxygen.

In preparation for landing, an astronaut on an earlier *Columbia* flight is helped into his pressure suit.

Out of Control

A similar investigation into the *Columbia* disaster revealed what happened to that spacecraft and crew in their final seconds. As the astronauts on *Columbia* were preparing to land, alarms began going off, warning of strain on the left wing and unusually high temperatures. The shuttle was pulling to the left as steering started to fail, and pieces began breaking off. Then, the shuttle lost communication with Mission Control and entered a steep, spinning dive that broke it apart. There were no survivors.

Drawing Conclusions

Experts who investigated the shuttle disasters discovered that both were caused by equipment failures. However, experts also found problems with NASA and the way it was run. After the *Challenger* explosion, President Ronald Reagan set up the Rogers **Commission** to find out what had gone wrong. The commission published its report on June 6, 1986. Officially, the disaster was blamed on the faulty O-ring. But the commission also wanted to know why the problem with the O-ring had been missed and why NASA managers had let the mission go ahead.

This piece of *Challenger's* rocket booster was found after the accident.

William Rogers *(left)* and Sally Ride *(second left)* were among those who examined pieces of the rocket booster.

Better Safety

The commission called for changes in the designs of rocket boosters and O-rings. It also asked NASA to improve the safety features on space shuttles and urged NASA managers to listen more carefully to the concerns and warnings of engineers and space experts. The space shuttle program was halted until the commission's report was studied and could be acted upon.

THE ROGERS COMMISSION

The Rogers Commission was led by William Rogers, a former politician. The other members included retired astronauts who knew the space program well. Neil Armstrong, who was the first person to walk on the moon, and Sally Ride, the first American woman astronaut, were members. So was Richard Feynman, a well-known scientist who won the 1965 Nobel Prize in Physics.

The members of the *Columbia* Accident Investigation Board visited the hangar where pieces of the destroyed shuttle were laid out.

More to Learn

The *Columbia* disaster showed that lessons from *Challenger* had not been learned. Just four hours after *Columbia* exploded, NASA set up the *Columbia* Accident Investigation Board (CAIB). The board's job was to find out what had caused the disaster and to report on what could be done to make future missions safer. The CAIB quickly confirmed that the cause of the disaster was the foam that had broken off the external fuel tank. The foam had damaged heat tiles, allowing hot gas to pour into *Columbia* as it returned to Earth.

FIXING PROBLEMS IN FLIGHT

Even though NASA knew that the foam had hit the shuttle and damaged heat tiles at liftoff, there was no way for anyone to fix the problem or even see it clearly. The CAIB said astronauts should be trained to do spacewalks to repair damage on the outside of shuttles. It also said the spacecraft's cameras should be upgraded to better detect and analyze shuttle damage.

NASA Criticized

After the CAIB report was released, NASA again received criticism. Before the *Columbia* explosion, the government had cut money from NASA's budget, yet the number of spaceflights had increased. As a result, managers were more focused on saving money and sticking to schedules than making sure spacecraft were safe. The board said NASA needed more money and support in addition to a new shuttle system that would replace its aging fleet.

A piece of insulation foam like this one was responsible for the tragic loss of *Columbia* and its crew.

The End of an Era

The *Columbia* disaster was the beginning of the end of the space shuttle program. In 2004, President George W. Bush said the shuttle program would stop once the International Space Station (ISS) was completed.

The majority of the construction on the ISS was finished by 2011.

INTERNATIONAL SPACE STATION

Space agencies from different countries helped build the ISS. The first part was launched in 1998, and more sections were added over the years. One of the space shuttles' main jobs had been to carry ISS sections into space and to take astronauts to and from the station.

Remembering

The shuttle program ended in 2011. During its 30-year history, shuttles made 135 flights, transported 355 people from 16 different countries, and delivered specialized equipment to space. The brave astronauts from the *Challenger* and *Columbia* missions have never been forgotten. **Asteroids** and moon **craters** have been named after them, and Christa McAuliffe continues to inspire students. More than three dozen schools around the world have been named after her.

FRANCIS "DICK" SCOBEE
MICHAEL J SMITH
ELLISON S ONIZUKA
JUDITH A RESNIK

RONALD E MCNAIR
S CHRISTA MCAULIFFE
GREGORY B JARVIS

NASA's annual Day of Remembrance event honors astronauts who have died in the name of space exploration.

KEY DATES

1986

January 28

11:38 a.m. *Challenger* launches and then explodes 73 seconds later.

February 6 The Rogers Commission is formed to investigate the disaster.

March 7 Divers find the wreckage of the crew cabin.

June 6 The Rogers Commission Report is released.

2003

January 16

10:39 a.m. *Columbia* launches.

February 1

8:44 a.m. *Columbia* reenters Earth's atmosphere.

8:59 a.m. Mission Control loses contact with the shuttle.

9:00 a.m. The orbiter starts to break up.

1:15 p.m. NASA sets up the CAIB.

August 26 The CAIB publishes its report.

QUIZ

How much have you learned about the space shuttle disasters? It's time to test your knowledge! Then, check your answers on page 32.

1. **Which was the first shuttle to be completed?**
   a) *Enterprise*
   b) *Columbia*
   c) *Atlantis*

2. **What was unusual about the weather on the day *Challenger* launched?**
   a) it was very hot
   b) it was very wet
   c) it was very cold

3. **What was the ring that caused the *Challenger* disaster?**
   a) D-ring
   b) O-ring
   c) S-ring

4. **What happened to *Columbia* upon reentry into the atmosphere?**
   a) Its rockets fell off.
   b) It overheated and broke apart.
   c) Fuel on the craft exploded.

5. **When did the space shuttle program end?**
   a) 2007
   b) 2009
   c) 2011

GLOSSARY

aerodynamic forces forces that act on something moving through air

aeronautics the science concerning building and flying aircraft and spacecraft

ascent the act of rising or climbing upward

asteroids small rocky objects that move around the sun

astronauts people who are trained to travel into space

atmosphere the thick layer of gases that surrounds Earth

boosters parts of a rocket that creates the power needed for liftoff and the first part of the flight

commission a group of experts that is put together to make an official investigation

craters bowl-shaped cavities on the surface of a planet or other space body, such as the moon

debris the pieces left when something breaks up or is destroyed

hangar a large building that houses aircraft or spacecraft

missions trips that have a particular task

mission specialists NASA astronauts who have been assigned to a particular mission to perform certain tasks

orbiter the part of a space shuttle where the crew lived and worked and where equipment was stored

payload specialists people who fly on a mission to carry out a particular job

satellites machines put into space that circle Earth and perform tasks such as taking photos, collecting weather information, and transmitting radio and TV signals

seal a part of a machine or object that stops gases and liquids from mixing together where parts join

test pilot a pilot who has taken additional training to be able to test new aircraft

INDEX

READ MORE

Kortemeier, Todd. *The Space Shuttle Challenger* (*Engineering Disasters*). Minneapolis: Abdo Publishing, 2020.

Loh-Hagan, Virginia. *Exploration and Explosion: Columbia Space Shuttle Disaster* (*Behind the Curtain*). Ann Arbor, MI: Cherry Lake Publishing, 2022.

Naujokaitis, Pranas T. *The Challenger Disaster: Tragedy in the Skies* (*History Comics*). New York: First Second, 2020.

LEARN MORE ONLINE

1. Go to **www.factsurfer.com** or scan the QR code below.

2. Enter **"Mission Explosions"** into the search box.

3. Click on the cover of this book to see a list of websites.

Answers to the quiz on page 30

1) A; 2) C; 3) B; 4) B; 5) C